BUFFALO RAILROADS
THROUGH TIME

STEPHEN G. MYERS

AMERICA
THROUGH TIME®
ADDING COLOR TO AMERICAN HISTORY

To my grandchildren, Jacob, Rebekah, and Anthony, who have suffered through so many train rides with their grandpa.

COVER PHOTOS:
Front cover, top: Geoff Gerstung
Front cover, bottom: Adam Vester
Back cover, top: Lower Lakes Marine Historical Society
Back cover, bottom: Don Rohauer

America Through Time is an imprint of Fonthill Media LLC
www.through-time.com
office@through-time.com

Published by Arcadia Publishing by arrangement with Fonthill Media LLC
For all general information, please contact Arcadia Publishing:
Telephone: 843-853-2070
Fax: 843-853-0044
E-mail: sales@arcadiapublishing.com
For customer service and orders:
Toll-Free 1-888-313-2665

www.arcadiapublishing.com

First published 2020

Copyright © Stephen G. Myers 2020

ISBN 978-1-68473-006-3

Typeset in Mrs Eaves XL Serif Narrow
Printed and bound in England

INTRODUCTION

The Buffalo area is a region filled with a variety of railroads and rail enthusiasts. From rail photographers to train watchers, scenic railroad riders to model railroaders, Buffalo has them all. Each one has their own unique story of how they became a railroad buff and the tales vary from grandpa or dad working on the rails, growing up trackside, or that first time they were asked up into the cab of a locomotive or caboose. That bug known as enthusiast, buff, or foamer just grabbed their heart from that moment and has held on ever since.

From riding the scenic excursion railroads in the area on the Arcade & Attica Railroad, the Buffalo Cattaraugus & Jamestown Scenic Railway, or along the Falls Road with the Medina Railroad Museum, we are brought back in time to an era when railroads were king and ruled the countryside. A visit to the Western New York Railway Historical Society's Heritage Discovery Center, Niagara Frontier Chapter of the National Railway Historical Society's Freight House and Museum, or the Central Terminal Restoration Corporation's iconic Buffalo Central Terminal are all part of today's railroad scene. Even the historic Williamsville Depot or Orchard Park Depot have been preserved to enrich their communities and share the local railroad history.

It has been nearly 190 years since the citizens of Buffalo wrote to the governor requesting a railroad be built there. Once it began to be built, it changed the face of Buffalo. Main lines were built, branch lines and yards, tracks into industries, lines up to grain elevators and over into the port and docks. The transfer of goods from grain, lumber, coal, coke, and steel moved from rail to freighter on Lake Erie. Buffalo was growing, and along with it, the railroad. Eventually, twenty-seven different railroad companies served the Buffalo area.

Building, milling, and manufacturing were all taking place in an ever-growing city and a large percentage of the population became employed by the railroad industry. Large freight yards took up swaths of land in and around the city, humming and bustling both day and night with the switching and screeching of rail cars as they banged into each other making up new trains to travel to faraway destinations. Smoke billowed from railroad roundhouses and shops as men labored each day hammering, riveting, and repairing the cars and locomotives so that the trains could keep rolling.

Moving people was another necessity to make travel year-round and to increase speeds. Travel by stagecoach on the turnpike or by pack boats on the canal was slow and tedious. With the advent of the railroad as a year-round transportation system, greater speed was developed. Uncomfortable and rustic at first, train travel became safe and timesaving. Then, a tragedy occurred that is still remembered today in the Buffalo area. The Angola Horror, as it came to be called, took place in December of 1867, when on a dark winter day, the New York Express heading to Buffalo derailed as it crossed over Big Sister Creek in Angola, NY. The last two cars fell into the icy creek below, resulting in the deaths of forty-nine passengers. Still the best way to travel, passenger trains improved with comfort, speed, and safety.

Railroad companies named their trains to advertise their scenery and amenities. Beautiful stations were constructed in Buffalo including the DL&W Terminal built at the foot of Main Street in 1917, the Lehigh Valley Terminal at 125 Main Street in 1916, and the New York Central's Buffalo Central Terminal in 1929 at the current Paderewski Drive, which was one of America's busiest train stations for fifty years. Other quaint stations were built of wood or stone in and around the city to fill the needs of the railroads and the traveling public. One railroad term for passenger trains was varnish. This differentiated the clean and modern passenger cars from those that hauled freight. The advertising departments created names for each train such as The Black Diamond, The Phoebe Snow, The Empire State Express, or the 20th Century Limited. Each symbolized their greatness and now live on in the annals of history.

It was Buffalo's industrial might and the great company names in railroading that made a huge impact in supplying the United States and her allies with aircraft, steel, and other items needed to sustain a nation through war. They supplied a military for victory along with the streams of sailors and soldiers riding troop trains to far off bases to prepare to protect their country. Buffalo railroads through time have had such an impact on the world and the nation, from being the second largest rail hub in the United States to its vital importance today. Buffalo is still a railroad center with several Amtrak passenger trains passing through her bounds each day, two Canadian railroads, two eastern class one railroads and a handful of regional and short line companies that move our materials, products and food through Buffalo and across a continent to provide for the needs of countless homes and families.

NEW YORK CENTRAL SYSTEM: The New York Central had the largest presence in the Buffalo area and from the Bailey Avenue Bridge, one could look down into the yard at the former West Shore Roundhouse with several steam locomotives being prepared for their next assignment. Today, the North Yard section of Frontier Yard can be seen with the Bailey Avenue Tower now removed. [*Top: Brian R. Wroblewski collection; Bottom: Author's photo*]

NEW YORK CENTRAL SYSTEM: The yard off Broadway was then known as the East Buffalo Yard and the DL&W Railroad Bridge crossed above. Today the yard is operated by CSX and is named Frontier Yard since it opened in 1957. The bridge abutments of the old DL&W are still in place, but the bridge and tracks are long since gone. CSX closed the Frontier Hump in 2009. [*Top: Brian R. Wroblewski collection; Bottom: Author's photo*]

NEW YORK CENTRAL SYSTEM: From the Harlem Road Bridge looking west into the East Buffalo Yard in 1953, the four-track main line along Broadway is active with two eastbound trains while the yard to the right will become the Frontier Yard and the Hump in a few short years. In a modern view, a CSX eastbound van train passes the yard after changing crews at Old Broadway. [*Top: Brian R. Wroblewski collection; Bottom: Author's photo*]

NEW YORK CENTRAL SYSTEM: Looking from the Harlem Road Bridge is a tree-lined Broadway Street and a train of new automobiles rolling east. Looking into the yard is the new and modern Frontier Yard. The former hump tower can be seen and the control tower is to the left. In a current view, a CSX train enters the South Yard from the east. [*Top: G. Hhre photo, WNYRHS collection; Bottom: Author's photo*]

NEW YORK CENTRAL SYSTEM: Buffalo Central Terminal can be seen through the smoke in the background on a busy railroad compared with today's diesel locomotives idling at the CSX Frontier Yard awaiting their next assignments on a snowy day. Then and now it is an around-the-clock operation. [*Top: Jeremy Taylor photo, NYCSHS collection; Bottom: Author's photo*]

NEW YORK CENTRAL SYSTEM: From the west end of the East Buffalo Yard, a steam locomotive is seen making its way from the roundhouse and will tie onto a train and depart the Queen City. The last remaining roundhouse in Buffalo is still used by a local business and once housed the Wagner Palace Car Company and later the Pullman Company until 1959. The roundhouse is located on Broadway behind Tops Market. The former Pennsylvania roundhouse is also still in use by Ebenezer Railcar Services in West Seneca. [*Top: Jim Van Brocklin photo; Bottom: Author's photo*]

NEW YORK CENTRAL SYSTEM: From the Harlem Road Bridge is the former West Shore Line Walden Avenue Yard. The field to the left will become the massive Frontier Yard. Now it has become a materials storage area for Frontier Yard and most of the trackage has been removed. [*Top: Brian R. Wroblewski collection; Bottom: Author's photo*]

NEW YORK CENTRAL SYSTEM: From Losson Road, one could get a view of the old Gardenville Yards and watch cars being pushed up the hump and sorted into new trains. Gardenville was an important yard for the Central until the opening of the modern Frontier Yard. [*Both photos: Brian R. Wroblewski collection*]

NEW YORK CENTRAL SYSTEM: The big Gardenville Yard in 1953 was filled with a variety of power from different locomotive manufacturers such as EMD out of LaGrange, IL, and ALCO in Schenectady, NY, all built in the 1940s and early 50s. Even a Lima Built J-2c Hudson from 1931 can be seen to the far right of the bottom photo. [*Both photos: Brian R. Wroblewski collection*]

NEW YORK CENTRAL SYSTEM: A Fairbanks-Morse CFA-20-4 leads a train of Pacemaker box cars through a neglected Gardenville Yard showing a lot of empty and weed covered tracks. This is a stark contrast to the now green fields that once were a massive railroad hub. [*Top: Stephan M. Koenig collection; Bottom: Author's photo*]

NEW YORK CENTRAL SYSTEM: EMD E8 number 4089 waits to depart Buffalo Central Terminal in a better era for the east side of the city of Buffalo, railroading in general, and Central Terminal. Below is the current operator CSX with a safety train to teach firemen and first responders about hazardous materials by rail in 2014. [*Top: Geoff Gerstung photo; Bottom: Adam Vester photo*]

NEW YORK CENTRAL SYSTEM: At track level a carman has been doing repair work to some cars as a blast of steam is released from an era when passenger cars were steam heated. Central Terminal today sits empty and has no railroad activity, but is still impressive as a CSX Q15701 double stack train rolls past in 2010. [*Top: Bruce Heatley photo; Bottom: Adam Vester photo*]

NEW YORK CENTRAL SYSTEM: A happy group is lined up in front of Buffalo Central Terminal with their cars and a sign in the window advertises the World's Fair in a vibrant era of the building. Currently the building hosts special events on occasion; one is being set up in the lower photo. [*Top: Nathan Vester collection; Bottom: Author's photo*]

NEW YORK CENTRAL SYSTEM: Near the end of train service at Buffalo Central, a lone RDC set is seen awaiting departure in 1979. In October of 1979, Amtrak would pull out of the station and rail service would stop. Looking out the window from the terminal, a CSX freight passes the abandoned platforms that were once bustling with passengers. [*Top: Author's photo; Bottom: Nathan Vester photo*]

NEW YORK CENTRAL SYSTEM: Inside the Central Terminal in July of 1979, the facility still shows its beauty, although service will end in a few short months. A 2019 train show was held in the terminal for railroad modelers, collectors and enthusiasts. Even after the neglect of decades, the building is still intriguing. [*Author's photos*]

NEW YORK CENTRAL SYSTEM: Built in 1929 and towering over East Buffalo, Central Terminal was constructed to handle 200 trains a day and provided offices and workstations for 1,500 employees. Men were busy dispatching trains and were paid good wages. Below is a recent annual train show in the terminal. [*Top: Bruce Heatley collection; Bottom: Author's photo*]

NEW YORK CENTRAL SYSTEM: From trainmasters, clerks, dispatchers, and other railroad positions that worked around the clock every day of the year, the building was eventually abandoned and fell into disrepair and neglected by owners. The Union News Company booth is lit up for a train show as once again life fills the historic building. [*Top: Author's collection; Bottom: Author's photo*]

New York Central System: After World War II with the further development and lowering costs of owning an automobile, building convenient expressways such as the New York State Thruway and the local Skyway, passenger traffic dwindled and the need for such a large station was not necessary. An old cart is displayed by the street exit at Central Terminal as festivals and events now bring groups of people into the station. [*Top: Bruce Heatley collection; Bottom: Author's photo*]

NEW YORK CENTRAL SYSTEM: From railroad workers to travelers, the building was once filled with people heading on their journeys. Empty ticket booths and no passengers became the norm as people flocked to the newly built airports or chose to drive their cars. Now the terminal is filled with shoppers at a recent train show. [*Top: Author's collection; Bottom: Author's photo*]

NEW YORK CENTRAL SYSTEM: As the world of railroading was rapidly changing, the demise of steam locomotives quickly switched to diesel power and the loss of passengers left railroad companies with a hefty bill to support aging infrastructure. Large facilities and a massive payroll all needed to be reduced as soon as possible and many times with little thought. Elevators that have sat silent for decades sit stalled on the bottom floor currently. [*Top: Bruce Heatley collection; Bottom: Author's photo*]

NEW YORK CENTRAL SYSTEM: An American Locomotive Company Schenectady, NY, built Niagara 4-8-4 steam locomotive number 6017 pulls a passenger train eastward through Buffalo in 1946. While a new locomotive, it would be retired in nine short years. Tower 49, outside of Buffalo Central Terminal, is seen below. [*Top: Jeffrey Nugent collection; Bottom: Bruce Heatley collection*]

NEW YORK CENTRAL SYSTEM: Company officers and dignitaries pose for a photograph at Niagara Yard alongside of an ALCO RS3 locomotive number 5205 in the early 1960s. The car shop can be seen in the distance and the yard tower is still in place. Below is a view of Niagara Yard as it looks at this time. [*Top: G. Hhre photo, WNYRHS collection; Bottom: Author's photo*]

NEW YORK CENTRAL SYSTEM: The small car shop at Niagara Yard has not changed much since the early 1960s, but the names on the freight cars certainly have. This recent view of the shop along with the locomotive service tracks are to the right. The car shop has recently been closed and is no longer in use. [*Top: G. Hhre photo, WNYRHS collection; Bottom: Author's photo*]

NEW YORK CENTRAL SYSTEM: A beautiful Central passenger train speeds by the Peace Bridge heading to Buffalo in 1947. The locomotive is a Hudson type but is seen steaming along the Niagara. In 1981, an Amtrak train is seen near the same location as she travels from Niagara Falls to make the next stop at Buffalo. [*Top: Charles Erler photo; Bottom: Don Rohauer photo*]

NEW YORK CENTRAL SYSTEM: Heading westbound for Detroit out of the Exchange Street station, the Michigan Avenue Bridge is in the background in 1953. Below, an Amtrak train has stopped at Exchange Street to pick up passengers in 2019. The station has since been demolished and a new station is under construction. [*Top: Albert Kerr photo, Niagara Frontier NRHS collection; Bottom: Author's photo*]

NEW YORK CENTRAL SYSTEM: Two EMD diesels rush through Buffalo with hopper cars as they pass by City Hall. Near the same location and a few decades later is an Amtrak train rolling through the city in June of 1992 with a Canadian Via Rail locomotive as a second unit. [*Top: Lower Lakes Marine Historical Society photo; Bottom: Don Rohauer photo*]

NEW YORK CENTRAL SYSTEM: A train full of passengers glides through Black Rock led by a Schenectady-built Alco Hudson as it crosses the Erie's International Branch on the way to Niagara Falls. The swing bridge is in the open position allowing a boat to go through and any trains will be held at the red signal. [*Top: Tom Mulaniff photo; Bottom: Author's photo*]

NEW YORK CENTRAL SYSTEM: Switcher number 877 is seen doing work at Michigan Avenue in Buffalo as the new Skyway construction progresses around 1953. CSX 2798 is serving a customer on Katherine Street before returning to the Ohio Street Yard with the empty cars. [*Top: Strong collection, Lower Lakes Marine Historical Society; Bottom: Author's photo*]

NEW YORK CENTRAL SYSTEM: Passengers await the arrival of their train at Westfield, New York, as a Buffalo bound train speeds by. To the left is the Jamestown Westfield & Northwestern trolley. Below, an empty Conrail coal train passes the Westfield station. Not only are there no longer passengers there, but few, if any, coal trains pass by. [*Top: Harold Ahlstrom photo; Bottom: Greg Lund photo*]

ERIE RAILROAD: Over on the Erie's East Buffalo Yard, a train rolls into the yard with the DL&W seen in the background. A brakeman below is seen walking back to the hump to ride another car down the tracks in an era when a railroad career was much more dangerous. [*Both photos: James Rowan photo, WNYRHS collection*]

ERIE RAILROAD: Pulling pins on the hump around 1942 is taking place at the East Buffalo Yard. Below, as a pin puller checks his switch list, a fellow railroader livens up the picture with some horseplay. The yard is busy with war-time traffic and many railroad men will soon be receiving draft notices. [*Both photos: James Rowan photo, WNYRHS collection*]

ERIE RAILROAD: An Erie brakeman rides a box car down the East Buffalo hump and the stock yards along with Central Terminal are in the background. Below, a Canadian Pacific train sits at the Norfolk Southern SK Yard with Central Terminal looming in the distance. [*Top: James Rowan photo, WNYRHS collection; Bottom: Author's photo*]

ERIE RAILROAD: A brakeman displays the finer points of his job as he clubs down the brake from the top of a box car. A railroad man crosses the tracks at the East Buffalo Yard with IQ Tower behind him. The clothing and the working conditions have changed drastically over the years. [*Both photos: James Rowan, WNYRHS collection*]

ERIE RAILROAD: Looking down into the yard, steam engines are belching out smoke as they sort the cars. Three railroaders pose for a picture at the yard in the early 1940s. The man in the middle is probably a carman with a hook in his hand to pull lids on the journal boxes. [*Both photos: James Rowan, WNRHS collection*]

ERIE RAILROAD: A winter scene looking down into the Erie East Buffalo Yard on a cold day during World War II. A Norfolk Southern engine idles at SK Yard looking near the approximate location of the old East Buffalo Yards. [*Top: James Rowan, WNRHS collection; Bottom: Author's photo*]

ERIE RAILROAD: Trackmen are hard at work clearing snow from the switches at East Buffalo in the early 1940s, a tough job for sure. At this time, the yard is gone and UPS has built their sorting facility there, but the sounds of railroading still surround the area with the Norfolk Southern so close. [*Top: James Rowan, WNRHS collection; Bottom: Author's photo*]

ERIE RAILROAD: A clean and beautiful Baldwin locomotive is tied down near Clinton and Babcock in Buffalo for a NRHS excursion in the mid-1950s. The engineer watches carefully as everyone departs the train so that no one catches a high heel on a rail. Close by and decades later is the Norfolk Southern SK Yard with NS power ready to lead a train east. [*Top: Joseph Gerenser photo, Niagara Frontier Chapter NRHS collection; Bottom: Author's photo*]

ERIE RAILROAD: An Erie Berkshire number 3397 is heading train 75 steaming through Hamburg on its westward journey in 1950 as it flies across a quiet crossing. In 2019, the Buffalo Southern prepares to bring the fair train into town using Montreal Locomotive Works C424 number 4212, built in 1965. [*Top: Jeffrey Nugent collection; Bottom: Author's photo*]

ERIE RAILROAD: In the summer of 1949, Erie number 3194 speeds west past the Hamburg Station as the sounds of her engine and the clanking cars following behind awakens the neighborhood. Seventy years later, a light engine moves on the Buffalo Southern approaching a vacant Hamburg Station. [*Top: O. H. Van Brocklin photo; Bottom: Author's photo*]

ERIE RAILROAD: The station agent has come out with two kerosene cans to fill the lanterns at the Walden Avenue Station on the Erie. Below is an Amtrak train arriving at the Buffalo Depew Station. Only Amtrak offers rail passenger service since private railroad companies gave it up in 1971. [*Top: Steamtown National Historic Site, Erie Railroad collection; Bottom: Author's photo*]

ERIE RAILROAD: The Erie's Depew station was on the east side of Transit Road. Below is the Depew Amtrak station with a Rohr Turboliner ready to depart. Depew is named after Chauncey M. Depew, president of the New York Central and Hudson River Railroad Company, which built the railroad shops there. [*Top: Steamtown National Historic Site, Erie Railroad collection; Bottom: Geoff Gerstung photo*]

ERIE RAILROAD: Crossing Oliver Street in North Tonawanda with the EL 2 Tower to the left, the Erie Lackawanna train led by a GP7 rolls south, in 1972. On the bottom is a recent photo of the EL-2 Tower owned by the Niagara Frontier Chapter of the NRHS. [*Top: Michael S. Lopat collection; Bottom: Author's photo*]

ERIE RAILROAD: In 1949, the Erie operated a steam excursion to the Kinzua Viaduct, led by the Mikado 3214 passing the JU Crossover in Buffalo. The Kinzua Viaduct was built by the Elmira Bridge Company in 1882, rebuilt in 1900 and collapsed in 2003. A CSX train passes under the Elk Street Bridge in Buffalo near the Honeywell facility. [*Top: Tom Mulaniff; Bottom; Author's photo*]

ERIE RAILROAD: Rolling past CB Junction in Cuba, New York, in 1949, this nearly two-year-old ALCO FA-1 leads a long freight with little effort and is among the most handsome style diesel locomotives ever designed. Still using ALCO locomotives in the area, the Western New York & Pennsylvania does some switching in Cuba. [*Top: Jeffrey Nugent collection; Bottom: Mike Stellpflug photo*]

DELAWARE LACKAWANNA & WESTERN RAILROAD: The beautiful terminal opened in 1917, helping to show the wealth and importance of the Buffalo area along with its value as a major railroad hub. Looking towards the site of the station and the USS *Little Rock* is the HSBC Arena to the left with General Mills to the right. [*Top: Steamtown National Historic Site, Erie Railroad collection; Bottom: Author's collection*]

DELAWARE LACKAWANNA & WESTERN RAILROAD: With the tripod set up and camera ready, train buffs have been trackside waiting for a great photograph for many decades now. On the platform of the DL&W, EMD SW1 locomotive number 431, built in 1940, takes a short break with the crew on board. Below are the remains of the DL&W train shed in the summer of 1979. [*Top; Strong collection, Lower Lakes Marine Historical Society; Bottom: Author's photo*]

DELAWARE LACKAWANNA & WESTERN RAILROAD: With a Lackawanna switcher shoving the cars to the platform on a rainy day, a Railway Express Agency car is also seen in the top photo and was a package delivery service much like UPS of today. REA was co-owned by many of the railroad companies. In the bottom photo, the famed Phoebe Snow departs Buffalo as the steam heat can be seen blowing from the last car. [*Both photos: Strong collection, Lower Lakes Marine Historical Society*]

DELAWARE LACKAWANNA & WESTERN RAILROAD: Above, the DL&W EMD E8A locomotive number 811, built in 1951, rolls past the Michigan Street Tower. Switching below, the Michigan Street Tower is EMD SW1 number 432, built in 1940. This area looks incredibly different today. [*Both photos: Strong collection, Lower Lakes Marine Historical Society*]

Delaware Lackawanna & Western Railroad: Enthusiasts gather around a steam run at the DL&W Terminal to see the Nickel Plate 175 Excursion in 1958. Below is the Nickel Plate Berkshire number 726 in 1957 on the Buffalo Junction Turntable. [*Top: Strong collection, Lower Lakes Marine Historical Society; Bottom: Fred B. Furminger photo*]

DELAWARE LACKAWANNA & WESTERN RAILROAD: Handsome EMD power is being fueled and sanded at the service center. Below is a cold winter day at Bison yard with the day's power waiting for its assignment. Today's modern locomotives may be cleaner and offer more comfort, but railroading is still a never-ending operation despite the time of day or weather. [*Top: M. J. Wronski, John Brahaney collection; Bottom: Author's photo*]

Delaware Lackawanna & Western Railroad: A shot taken around 1955, from the DL&W East Buffalo Tower, has number 603 in the lead, an EMD FTA built in May of 1945. Norfolk Southern EMD SD40E takes a break at the Buffalo SK Yard with the former New York Central's Buffalo Central Terminal still standing tall in the background. [*Top; M. J. Wronski photo; Bottom: Author's photo*]

LEHIGH VALLEY RAILROAD: This majestic terminal building opened on August 29, 1916, and served the city until its closing on August 11, 1955. In 1960, the building was demolished and the William J. Donovan State Office Building was constructed on the site. Phillips Lytle and Courtyard by Marriott now occupy the property that was once a bustling station. The NFTA Metro Rail still gives some semblance of rail service here. [*Top: Richard Ganger photo; Bottom: Author's photo*]

LEHIGH VALLEY RAILROAD: Buffalo was the western terminus of the Lehigh Valley and an important city for a railroad connection. This route was also called the Black Diamond Route since the purpose was to move anthracite coal out of the Pennsylvania coal mines. Moving passengers was also railroad business as seen in this picture of a train departing the Buffalo Terminal. Today CSX and Norfolk Southern both operate intermodal terminals in Buffalo. [*Top: Richard Ganger photo; Bottom: Author's photo*]

LEHIGH VALLEY RAILROAD: Famed trains like The Black Diamond and The Maple Leaf sped across the Lehigh Valley filled with businessmen, families and vacationers when train travel was the choice of transportation. The Buffalo Terminal had ten tracks. Seen here is an EMD diesel locomotive working to build passenger trains at the station. A newly designed Amtrak Acela train, built in Hornell, New York, crosses CP Draw on its way to Pueblo, Colorado, for testing. [*Top: Phil Soyring collection; Bottom: Author's photo*]

LEHIGH VALLEY RAILROAD: The deadline of the steam locomotives, having been replaced by diesels and now rendered useless and awaiting the scrapper's torch. A Canadian Pacific CP143 train passes under the long South Buffalo Railroad Bridge near Seneca Yard as the SB train crosses above, heading to Buffalo Creek Yard. [*Top: Richard Ganger photo; Bottom: Author's photo*]

LEHIGH VALLEY RAILROAD: At the Lehigh's Shops on South Ogden Street, 4-6-2 K3 Pacific Number 2058 receives coal and is being serviced for the next assignment. It is hard to believe that it is all gone, and now a CVS Pharmacy and Wendy's occupy the property. [*Top: Bob Andrycha collection; Bottom; Author's photo*]

LEHIGH VALLEY RAILROAD: Moving freight up to Niagara Falls, NY, with a 2-8-2 Mikado on the Lehigh, as she nears Suspension Bridge Yard in 1946. The Niagara River and Canadian border are off to the right. Amtrak awaits her departure from the new Niagara Falls, New York Station. [*Top: Jeffrey Nugent collection; Bottom: Author's photo*]

LEHIGH VALLEY RAILROAD: At the Tifft Street Yard in 1975, this view was of the Lehigh with a lash-up of three EMD GP38-2s ready for service. Looking from the Tifft Street Bridge into the Buffalo & Pittsburgh Buffalo Creek Yard is a broad view of the city skyline, along with the BP, NS, BSOR, and CSX railroads. [*Top: John Marriott photo; Bottom: Author's photo*]

PENNSYLVANIA RAILROAD: PRR 4-8-2 number 6835 is looking to tie onto the train as it passes under the Buffalo Central Terminal in 1952. The modern Pennsylvania operator Norfolk Southern has one of their trains on former New York Central, now CSX trackage, as they pass by the empty terminal. [*Top: John M. Prophet photo; Bottom: Nathan Vester photo*]

PENNSYLVANIA RAILROAD: Train 570 with a Baldwin 4-6-2 in charge is passing Tower 49 as she backs away from Central Terminal. A Norfolk Southern crew and power have grabbed the circus train from the CSX Frontier Yard and are heading to their own rails as they pass Central Terminal. In 2017, the Barnum & Bailey Circus Trains ceased to operate and the rail equipment was sold off. [*Top; John M. Prophet photo; Bottom: Nathan Vester photo*]

PENNSYLVANIA RAILROAD: The Skyway is nearing completion and will open in the fall of 1955 and construction continues as a lone Pennsy switcher and caboose sit below. There is still plenty of industry for railroads to serve in Buffalo. A CSX transportation job is seen setting off cars in a customer facility. [*Top: G. Strong, Lower Lakes Marine Historical Society photo; Bottom: Author's photo*]

PENNSYLVANIA RAILROAD: A Baldwin 4-8-2 rumbles south past the East Aurora Station in the 1940s. The silence is still broken here by an occasional freight train, but the passenger station is now under private ownership and operating as a restaurant. [*Top: Franklin Gnau photo, Niagara Frontier NRHS collection; Bottom: Author's photo*]

BALTIMORE & OHIO
RAILROAD: Leaving the DL&W
Buffalo Terminal, B&O train 251
starts her long trip to Pittsburgh
in 1952. A whole different scene
at this location is the NFTA Metro
train carefully making her way
past all the recent construction.
[*Top: R. G. Nugent photo; Bottom:
Author's photo*]

BALTIMORE & OHIO RAILROAD: Entering the Tifft Street Yards in 1969 is a mixed freight powered by all EMD F7 A and B units. A South Buffalo train makes her way down into the Buffalo Creek Yard while a Buffalo & Pittsburgh locomotive rolls under the bridge. [*Top: Francis G. LeTeste photo; Bottom: Author's photo*]

BALTIMORE & OHIO RAILROAD: In 1953, an NRHS Special stops at the Orchard Park Depot on her way to visit the Kinzua Bridge near Bradford, Pennsylvania. The station closed to passengers, but is maintained by the Western NY Railway Historical Society, is a museum and open for special events. The tracks south of the station have been removed and will become a bike trail. [*Top: Franklin Gnau photo; Bottom: Author's photo*]

BALTIMORE & OHIO RAILROAD: In a 1954 scene at the Springville Station, B&O train 251 readies for the run to Pittsburgh while in 1984, the Chessie System still ran freight on the line, but the station and passenger service were gone. Today, the track is a bike trail and the station vacant. [*Top: Richard Ganger photo; Bottom: Don Rohauer photo*]

BUFFALO CREEK: It is a cold day in the Creek's Yard as Engine 28 steams out. This was lucky for some of the trackside residents, as they could obtain a little coal for warmth from the local railroad stocks. Now abandoned and crumbling, the old Cargill Elevators sit quietly, but still tell the story of a much busier time at the Ohio Street Yard. [*Top: Richard Ganger photo; Bottom: Author's photo*]

BUFFALO CREEK: A Dunkirk built ALCO Number 26 makes a light move across the yard in 1938 and the city is busy with trains and ships, despite the Great Depression. A quiet summer scene of the CSX Ohio Street Yard, as number 2697 rolls back into the yard. [*Top: Richard Ganger photo; Bottom: Author's photo*]

BUFFALO CREEK: In a day of steam hissing and wooden box cars, so much of the work was done by laborers with strong backs. Men were kept busy loading train cars and trucks to keep the country fed. CSX is seen switching the General Mills Plant in a picture that appears much quieter and less labor intensive as in the past. The skies of Buffalo still have the sweet smell of Cheerios. [*Top: Western New York Heritage Press collection; Bottom: Author's photo*]

BUFFALO CREEK: Buffalo Creek ALCO S2 Number 45 spots cars at Great Lakes Freight with police presence during a strike. Unused and rusted rails lead into the grain silos in Buffalo in an area that was once busy with train cars moving in and out. The American Grain Elevator was built in 1906 and provided much business for the railroad. [*Top: WNYRHS collection; Bottom: Author's photo*]

BUFFALO CREEK: A line of vintage automobiles waits for the train to clear up at the General Mills plant. (Note the Buffalo Creek box cars with their flour sack logos). CSX serves the General Mills Plant currently from the Ohio Street Yard, moving strings of box cars and covered hoppers in and out of the plant. [*Top: Strong collection, Lower Lakes Marine Historical Society; Bottom: Don Rohauer photo*]

BUFFALO CREEK: Tracks were still in place to both bridges in 1974 as the Buffalo Creek crosses the river with a string of boxcars. The box cars were used to haul grain, and although the doors were coopered, plenty of grain would still fall out in the yards and rot, leaving a pungent odor. Then and now, plenty of deer and wild turkeys are spotted in the area eating what falls out of the cars. A Norfolk Southern multilevel train is seen crossing the bridge in 2019. [*Top: Ken Kraemer photo; Bottom: Author's photo*]

SOUTH BUFFALO RAILWAY: Built in 1948, this American Locomotive S2 switcher is two years old as it handles some gons (gondolas) of bridge girders in the Bethlehem Steel plant at Lackawanna, NY. A car mover spots some bad orders at the South Buffalo Shop for repairs. [*Top: Al Brose photo; Bottom: Author's photo*]

SOUTH BUFFALO RAILWAY: Looking into the yards off Lake Avenue at Tower D in July of 1953 and mounds of slag to the left, in many ways the area still looks the same. The yard is still active and a cold winter wind off Lake Erie makes for a chilly view as two switchers back into the yard and make up a train. [*Top: WNYRHS collection; Bottom: Author's photo*]

SOUTH BUFFALO RAILWAY: Pushing cars out onto the lake and dumping slag was a common occurrence, and during World War II, Bethlehem Steel was working full bore producing steel for the war effort. Loads of armor stone are being brought in to build up the Buffalo North and South Breakwater Walls. [*Top: Steel Plant Museum of Western New York; Bottom: Author's photo*]

SOUTH BUFFALO RAILWAY: The C furnace inside the plant with a steam locomotive is doing its chores. Although only a tiny fraction of what used to be in Buffalo, there are still some survivors in the area and they still load gondolas with steel. [*Top: Steel Plant Museum of Western New York; Bottom: Author's photo*]

SOUTH BUFFALO RAILWAY: The South Buffalo was the steel railroad of Buffalo, for it served the steel industries in that area. The railroad had tracks inside the Lackawanna Steel Plant known later as Bethlehem Steel, served the facility with raw materials and moved the finished products. Remnants of the old steel plants can still be seen, and tracks are still active to serve a few customers. [*Top: Steel Plant Museum of Western New York; Bottom: Author's photo*]

CHESAPEAKE & OHIO: Another image that will never be seen again as C&O handles a freight train at North Tonawanda and passes Oliver Street and the EL2 Tower in 1975. Two locomotives and cabooses are on display outside of the Niagara Frontier Chapter of the National Railway Historical Society in North Tonawanda. [*Top: Ken Kraemer photo; Bottom: Author's photo*]

CHESSIE SYSTEM: The Orchard Park Depot with images that will never happen again, as a Chessie System passes the depot in the winter of 1979. In May of 1996, the current owner of the tracks, the Buffalo & Pittsburgh Railroad, rolls past the Orchard Park Depot. Currently the line is only used to store rail cars and the track is removed from the depot south. [*Top: Ken Kraemer photo; Bottom: Don Rohauer photo*]

DELAWARE & HUDSON: The D&H Bicentennial locomotive leads a set of ALCO rebuilds on train Apollo 1 out of Bison Yard in 1976. Two Norfolk Southern EMDs pull a string of rusty salt cars east out of Bison Yard and hurry to double up their train before the storm hits. Much of the salt to keep the winter roads ice free come by rail from nearby Retsof, NY. [*Top: Devan Lawton photo; Bottom: Author's photo*]

DELAWARE & HUDSON: With ALCO and EMD power and the colors of the D&H, Boston & Maine, and Norfolk Western, a D&H train passes FW Tower in an era when Guilford Transportation offered some great lash-ups. A Norfolk Southern lone locomotive sits at Tifft Street in our present time when most engines are GEs, and the variety of colors and logos have greatly decreased. [*Top: photo Doug Kroll; Bottom: Author's photo*]

HANNA FURNACE: Number 14 was an EMD SW1 locomotive and worked the plant for many years until its closing in 1982. Today, the locomotive sits unused near the SK Yard in Buffalo at a scrap metal yard neglected and disgraced since her glory days are behind her. [*Top: Marty Mann photo; Bottom: Author's photo*]

PENN CENTRAL: With four PC EMD locomotives pulling a piggyback train in 1970 through South Buffalo, the company has about six more years before becoming Conrail. The Penn Central was a mismanaged mistake brought about by the merger of the New York Central and the Pennsylvania Railroads in 1968. The CSX Beilhack Rotary Snow Blower works its way through South Buffalo in the November 2014 blizzard. [*Top: John Marriott photo; Bottom: Author's photo*]

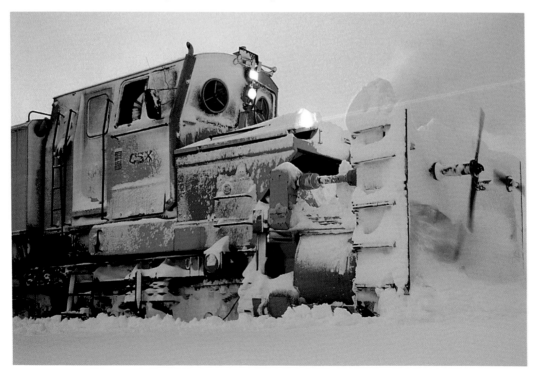

AMTRAK: United Aircraft's Turbotrain was originally owned by the Department of Transportation and visited Buffalo Central Terminal with another attempt to modernize passenger rail travel and increase speeds. In 2009, the television news show *Good Morning America* leased an Amtrak train to traverse the countryside and is seen passing by the Central Terminal. [*Top: Geoff Gerstung photo; Bottom: Adam Vester photo*]

AMTRAK: Central Terminal remained an active passenger train station until 1979. In 1976, New York State acquired the Rohr Turboliners that added a futuristic and unique look to Amtrak's Empire Service. Central Terminal still guards the East Side of Buffalo and lights up a dark rainy sky with a CSX geometry train waiting for its morning duties. [*Top: Geoff Gerstung photo; Bottom: Adam Vester photo*]

INTERNATIONAL BRIDGE: The bridge was built across the Niagara River to link Canada and the United States by rail and completed in 1873. It was originally built to be shared by several competing railroads and is now owned by the Canadian National Railway and sees about a dozen trains a day crossing the International Border. The N&W is seen entering into Fort Erie in 1969, compared to a modern double stack train entering the United States. [*Top: Ken Kraemer photo; Bottom: Authors photo*]

INTERNATIONAL BRIDGE: Before all of the big mergers and the formation of Conrail, a variety of railroads and color schemes led trains across the border, but even today there are still a few different company colors that pull freight across the Niagara River. A Wabash train rolls across the bridge in contrast to the Norfolk Southern train of today. The Wabash was absorbed into the N&W and finally into the current NS System. [*Top: Ken Kraemer photo; Bottom: Gregory Lund photo*]

NIAGARA JUNCTION RAILWAY: The railroad serviced industry in the Niagara Falls, New York, area with 11 miles of track and utilized electric locomotives for power until Conrail took over operations and replaced the electrics with diesels by 1978. The locomotive shop later became a private company to clean tank cars for the chemical industry. The site has changed ownership a few times and is presently active. [*Top: M. J. Wronski photo, John Brahaney collection; Bottom: Author's photo*]

CONSOLIDATED RAIL CORPORATION: The Lockport branch had a business train to show executives, politicians, and dignitaries the new Somerset Power Plant which was recently completed. The Somerset Plant along with a few customers were served on the line and interchange with the Falls Road Railroad at Lockport, NY. CSX still serves industry in the area with rail service, although the power plant is now inactive. [*Top: Neil Keirn photo; Bottom: Gregory Lund photo*]

ARCADE & ATTICA RAILROAD: The line handles both freight for local customers and excursion trains for passengers. The AA 118 steam locomotive was built by American Locomotive Company in 1920 and adds old time nostalgia when running passenger trains from Arcade to Curriers and back. [*Top: Patrick Connors collection; Bottom: Author's photo*]

ARCADE & ATTICA RAILROAD: Freight is the mainstay of a railroad company and moving freight keeps them in business. Locomotive AA 110 was built by General Electric at Erie, Pennsylvania, in 1941 and earned her keep by moving freight and passenger excursions and currently on display in the parking lot. AA 112 was built by GE in 1945 and still hauls trains for the railroad. [Top: Patrick Connors collection; Bottom: Author's photo]

ACKNOWLEDGMENTS

I would like to express my gratitude to the following institutions and individuals. Without their generous contributions and knowledge of Buffalo railroading this project could not be preserved.

This book would not have been possible without the kind help of the late Ronald Dukarm and the time that he spent with me at the Heritage Discovery Center in Buffalo and at his home. Special thanks go to the Western New York Railway Historical Society and the Niagara Frontier Chapter National Railway Historical Society, where the majority of these images were obtained and scanned. I would also like to acknowledge the assistance of Ron Dukarm, Ed Patton, Greg Gerstung, Jim Ball, Greg Lund, Devan Lawton, Charles Newton, Adam Vester, Nathan Vester, John Brahaney, Patrick Connors, Patrick Connors Jr, Brian Wroblewski, Bruce Heatley, Joe Kocsis, Don Rohauer, Mike Stellpflug, Ken Kraemer, Stephan Koenig, Lower Lakes Marine Historical Society, and the Steel Plant Museum of Western New York. Also, to my wife Marianne Myers, who without her patience and assistance none of this would be possible. Lest I forget, my grandchildren, Jacob, Rebekah, and Anthony, who have suffered through (and will continue to do so) more train adventures with their Grandpa.

This book is not intended to be an exhaustive history or a complete overview of all the area railroads and operations. It is rather to be enjoyed as a look at Buffalo railroading through our current times and past decades. You can still find railroad buffs trackside each day with camera in hand documenting the activity of the day with a smile and a friendly wave to the passing train crew.